Boots

Sacha Voit with Jessica Butcher

T0347850

methuen | drama

LONDON · NEW YORK · OXFORD · NEW DELHI · SYDNEY

METHUEN DRAMA
Bloomsbury Publishing Plc
50 Bedford Square, London, WC1B 3DP, UK
1385 Broadway, New York, NY 10018, USA

BLOOMSBURY, METHUEN DRAMA and the Methuen Drama logo are
trademarks of Bloomsbury Publishing Plc

First published in Great Britain 2019

Copyright © Sacha Voit and Jessica Butcher, 2019

Sacha Voit and Jessica Butcher have asserted their right under the Copyright,
Designs and Patents Act, 1988, to be identified as authors of this work.

For legal purposes the Acknowledgements on pp. 64–68
constitute an extension of this copyright page.

Cover design: Ben Anslow

Cover image © Crucible Creative

A catalogue record for this book is available from the British Library.

ISBN: PB: 978-1-3501-2565-0
ePDF: 978-1-3501-2566-7
eBook: 978-1-3501-2567-4

Series: Modern Plays

Typeset by Mark Heslington Ltd, Scarborough, North Yorkshire

To find out more about our authors and books visit
www.bloomsbury.com and sign up for our newsletters.

Old Bomb Theatre, All Ignite Theatre & The Bunker present

BOOTS

by

Sacha Voit with Jessica Butcher

Cast

Liz	**Amanda Boxer**
Willow	**Tanya Loretta Dee**

The performance lasts approximately 1 hour and 15 minutes.

Director	**Nadia Papachronopoulou**
Set and Costume Designer	**Lia Waber**
Lighting Designer	**Jack Weir**
Sound Designer	**Chris Drohan**
Stage Manager	**Ali Graham**
Movement Director	**Quang Kien Van**

AMANDA BOXER

Amanda was born in New York and trained at LAMDA. She won Best Actress in the London Fringe Awards for *Strange Snow* (Theatre Technis).

Theatre includes *The Blue Hour of Natalie Barney* (Arcola), *Mosquitoes* (National Theatre), *Babette's Feast* (The Print Room), *Blue Heart* (Tobacco Factory and Orange Tree Theatre), *Medea* (Almeida Theatre), *Uncle Vanya* (St James), *Prisoner of Second Avenue* (Vaudeville), *The Sea Plays* (Old Vic Tunnels), *The House of Bernarda Alba* (Gielgud Theatre), *The Graduate* (Gielgud Theatre), *A Touch of the Poet* (Young Vic and West End), *The Painter* (Arcola Theatre), *Macbeth* (Arcola Theatre), *The Destiny of Me* (Finborough Theatre), *Many Roads to Paradise* (Finborough Theatre), *The Arab Israeli Cookbook* (Gate and Tricycle Theatre), *The Pain and the Itch* (Royal Court), *The Strip* (Royal Court), *Cling To Me Like Ivy* (Birmingham Rep), *The Rivals* (Theatr Clwyd), *The Yiddish Queen Lear* (Southwark Playhouse and Bridewell), *Come Blow Your Horn* (Manchester Royal Exchange), *The Fall Guy* (Manchester Royal Exchange), *The Misanthrope* (Manchester Royal Exchange), *Absurd Person Sing*ular (Manchester Royal Exchange), *Way of the World* (Cambridge Theatre Company), *A State of Affairs* (The Duchess Theatre).

Television includes *Casualty*, *Miss Marple, Sense and Sensibility, Silent Witness*, *Doctors*, *Casualty*, *Bodies*, *The Shell Seekers*, *Trial and Retribution*, *Chalk*, *Road Rage*, *Goodbye My Love*, *Cider With Rosie*.

Film includes *Chatroom*, *Malice In Wonderland*, *Russian Dolls*, *Saving Private Ryan*, *Together*, *Things I Do For You*, *Bad Behaviour*.

TANYA LORETTA DEE

Tanya has just finished working with Paines Plough associate company 'Middle Child Theatre' playing lead role Kat in *One Life Stand* by Eve Nicol, which finished a successful run at Paines Plough Roundabout at Edinburgh Fringe, and continued with a UK National tour until October 2018.

She received the 'Highly Commended Award' for her performance as lead role Willow in *Boots* by Jessica Butcher and Sacha Voit at Vault Festival 2018.

Tanya played lead role Mickey/Emma Clarke, in Futures Theatre premier production of *Offside* by award-winning writers Sabrina Mahfouz and Hollie McNish, which toured across the UK and had a successful run at Edinburgh Fringe, Pleasance Theatre in 2017.

Other theatre includes *1867* (The Albany Theatre), *Marcel for Melody* (The Royal Court), *Scumbags* (Rosemary Branch), *Long Sentences* (The Albany) directed by Ellen McDougall and Deborah Pearson.

Television includes playing Tanya Harvey in *Law and Order UK* (ITV), as well being seen in *The Bill* (ITV), *In the Line of Beauty* (BBC 1), *EastEnders* (BBC 1) and various commercials for both ITV and Channel 4. Tanya also played the lead character Olivia in the feature film *Vehemence* by Meshack Enahoro.

Tanya is also a writer and poet, and was nominated Best Debut Performance Poet at the Zoo Awards, the longest-running poetry awards ceremony in London, as part of Farrago Poetry.

Tanya is currently writing her first play – due to be in production in 2019.

NADIA PAPACHRONOPOULOU

Nadia was the Emerging Director at National Theatre Wales and Resident Director at the Orange Tree Theatre and is currently working with the National Theatre as one of the NT connections directors.

As director credits include *Uncle Vanya* (National Tour), *After The Ball* (Gatehouse), *The Philanthropist:* Understudy Run (West End), *Mapping Brent* (Tricycle), *Non Essential Personnel* (Orange Tree), *Unrivalled Landscape* (Orange Tree), *Whisper Tree* (Pembroke Festival), *Recipe for a Perfect Wife* (Charing Cross and King's Head), *Nothing but Mammals* (Old Red Lion).

As assistant director credits include Tim Sheader on *A Tale of Two Cities* (Regents Park Theatre), Simon Callow on *The Philanthropist* (West End), Justin Audibert on *My Mother Medea* (Unicorn), Rachel Bagshaw on *The Shape of Pain* (Pulse Festival and Southbank Centre), Rachel Bagshaw on *Icons* (National Theatre Studio), Jo Davies on *Silly Kings* (National Theatre Wales), *Seven Year Twitch*, *Julius Caesar*, *The Man Who Pays the Piper*, *Sauce for the Goose*, *Love's Comedy*, *Yours for the Asking* (Orange Tree).

SACHA VOIT

Sacha Voit is a writer and theatre maker from Scotland who trained at the Scottish Youth Theatre and York University before making productions in Edinburgh, York and London. Sacha's first play won highly commended at Vault Festival 2018 and previous work has been nominated for four Off West End Awards including Best New Play and Best Production.

Theatre includes *Being Tommy Cooper* (Franklin Productions, National Tour), *The Church of IfEyeHad* (Bush Bazaar: Bush Theatre), *Twelfth Night* (Nursery Theatre), *Being Tommy Cooper* (Old Red Lion), *Talking in Bed* (Theatre503), *Bed, Pinter...esque, Hang Up*, *Waiting for Godot*, *Oleanna* (York Theatre Royal Studio), *Pitch Perfect* (Tristan Bates Theatre), *Edem* (Jermyn Street Theatre), *Taming of the Shrew* (C Venues, Edinburgh), *Office Song* (White Bear Theatre), *The Merchant of Venice*, *As You Like It* (York Shakespeare Company).

As associate director credits include *Shiverman* (Theatre 503), *Antigone* (Southwark Playhouse), *Fair Trade* (Shatterbox Theatre Company).

As assistant director credits include *Jeeves and Wooster Perfect Nonsense* (Mark Goucher, National Tour) *Yes, Prime Minister* (Mark Goucher, UK Tour), *Mary Shelley* (Shared Experience, UK Tour), *Three Days In May* (Trafalgar Studios and tour), *Lysistrata* (Rose Theatre, Kingston), *All I Want For Christmas* (Jermyn Street Theatre), *This Story Of Yours* (Old Red Lion Theatre), *Decade* (Theatre503), *Madagascar* (Primavera Productions), *Twelfth Night*, *The White Crow* (York Theatre Royal Studio).

JESSICA BUTCHER

Jessica is a writer and actor. She has an English Literature degree from King's College London and trained at Drama Studio London. Her first play *Sparks*, which she both wrote and performed, won Show of the Week at VAULT Festival 2018 and sold out at the Edinburgh Festival 2018, winning the Best Musical Award from Musical Theatre Review. She is currently writing her next musical with composer Anoushka Lucas.

She is also widely known for her role as Lucy Fuller in Camilla Whitehill's award-winning play *Where Do Little Birds Go?* (UK Tour, 2015; Edinburgh Festival 2015 and Old Red Lion Theatre, 2016).

Her theatre work includes *Offside* by Sabrina Mahfouz and Hollie McNish (UK Tour and Edinburgh Festival 2017).

Television includes *EastEnders* (BBC), *Vivaldi's Women* (BBC).

LIA WABER – SET AND COSTUME DESIGNER

Lia Camille Waber originally trained as a dressmaker and retrained at Central School of Speech and Drama in Design for Stage. After graduating she collaborated with Circus Fahraway as a costume designer and maker. She returned to work on productions at Central several times, including *PUSH* at the New Diorama and the set for *From Morning To Midnight*.

Waber has since worked and collaborated with contemporary opera makers for the Jerwood programme for writers, composers and directors in Aldeburgh and worked on a project about the composer Gustav Doret.

Other theatre design includes *The Crucible, DNA, A Servant to Two Masters* (Jacksons Lane), *Schrödinger's Dog* (White Bear Theatre).

JACK WEIR – LIGHTING DESIGNER

Jack trained at Guildhall School of Music and Drama and won the ETC award for Lighting Design in 2014.

He is a WhatsOnStage Award and two-time OffWestEnd Award nominee for Best Lighting Designer.

Recent lighting design includes *Grindr The Opera* (Above The Stag), *The Wizard of Oz* (Blackpool Opera House), *The Funeral Director* (Southwark Playhouse), *Rain Man* (UK tour), *The Boys in the Band* (Vaudeville Theatre), *Dust* (Trafalgar Studios), *Rothschild & Sons* (Park Theatre), *George's Marvellous Medicine* (Leicester Curve and Rose Theatre and UK tour), *Judy!* (Arts Theatre), *Assata Taught Me* (Gate Theatre), *The Plague* (Arcola Theatre), *Out Of Order* (Yvonne Arnaud Theatre and UK tour), *Pray So Hard For You* (Finborough Theatre), *Laronde* (Bunker Theatre), *Four Play* (Theatre503), *Summer In London* (Theatre Royal Stratford East), *Pyar Actually* (Watford Palace and tour), *Talk Radio* (Old Red Lion Theatre), *Holding The Man*, *Beautiful Thing*, *Maurice* (Above The Stag), *West Side Story* (Bishopsgate Institute).

CHRIS DROHAN – SOUND DESIGNER

Sound Design includes *New Nigerians* (Arcola and UK Tour), *The Paradise Circus* (The Playground Theatre), *Armour* (Vaults), *Harvey* (Playground), *Clockwork Canaries* (Theatre Royal Plymouth), *After the Ball* (Gatehouse), *All Or Nothing* (Ambassadors Theatre), *Knock Knock* (Tour), *Thrown* (Underbelly Edinburgh), *9 to 5* (Gatehouse), *Tenderly: The Rosemary Clooney Musical* (Wimbledon Studio), *What Shadows* (Edinburgh Lyceum, as Associate Sound Designer), *Ready Or Not* (UK Tour and Arcola Theatre), *The Mirror Never Lies* (Cockpit), *After Three Sisters* (Jack Studio Theatre), *Tonight at the Museum: Charlie Chaplin* (Cinema Museum), *Tis Pity* (Tristan Bates), *The Pursuit of Happiness* (RADA Festival), *Phoebe* (Kings Head Theatre), *The Marvellous Adventures of Mary Seacole* (Edinburgh Festival), *In The Gut* (Blue Elephant), *All Or Nothing* (Vaults Theatre and UK Tour), *The Lamellar Project* (UK Tour and Arcola Theatre), *Dr Angelus* (Finborough), *Don't Smoke in Bed* (Finborough), *The One Day of the Year* (Finborough), *Spring Awakening* (Chelsea Theatre), *Seussical* (Chelsea Theatre), *Resolution* (The Space and Etcetera Theatre), *The Drunken City* (Tabard Theatre), *Roaring Trade* (Park Theatre) *Finders Keepers* (Park Theatre), *Stiching* (White Bear), *Counting Stars* (Old Red Lion and Assembly Edinburgh), *The Social Notwork* (Lion and Unicorn and Camden Fringe), *La Boheme* (Arcola Theatre), *Shock Treatment* (Kings Head Theatre).

QUANG KIEN VAN – MOVEMENT DIRECTOR

Quang trained at Central School of Ballet in London.

Theatre as movement director includes *Forgotten* (Arcola Theatre), *Goats*, *Tottenham Symphony, Bunny Dance* (Royal Court), *Lunar Shadows* (QKV Projects), *SHAME: a double bill* (Bang Bang Bang Group), *Lunar Orbits, Lunar Corps* (Chinese Arts Space).

Theatre as performer includes *The Internet is Serious Business* (Royal Court), *Miaan*, *SisGo*, *Innocence* (Scottish Dance), *Blake Diptych* and *Disgo* (Darkin Ensemble), *View from the Shore* (Jacky Lansley Dance), *O* (Michael Clark Company), *Mystere* (Cirque du Soleil), Matthew Bourne's *Swan Lake* (Adventures in Motion Pictures).

Opera includes *Skin Deep* (Opera North), *Ariodante* (English National Opera).

ALI GRAHAM – STAGE MANAGER

Ali trained at LAMDA, graduating in 2010.

For the past two years she has been Company Stage and Production Manager at Fourth Monkey Actor Training Company.

Previous productions as stage manager include *A Christmas Carol* (National Tour), *Two's Company* (Scene & Heard), *Sparks* (Vaults Festival), *Boots* (Vaults Festival), *The Tempest* (Thick as Thieves and National Tour), *Macbeth* (Southwark Playhouse), *Angel Cake* (Camden People's Theatre), *Just So Stories* (Lost Theatre and Edinburgh Festival), *Childsplay* (National Tour), *Being Tommy Cooper* (Old Red Lion Theatre and National Tour).

Previous productions as deputy stage manager include *Robinson Crusoe* (The MTA) and Fourth Monkey Theatre Company.

ALL IGNITE THEATRE

All Ignite makes relevant, unexpected theatre. It was founded by director Jelena Budimir and producer Sanna-Karina Aab after they met on *White Guy on the Bus* – an acclaimed production at the Finborough Theatre.

Other theatre includes *Beast on the Moon* (Finborough Theatre).

OLD BOMB THEATRE

Old Bomb Theatre Company began in 2016 with David Mamet's *Oleanna*. Since then it has gone on to make award-winning shows in Yorkshire, Edinburgh and London. The OBTC's purpose is to show that theatre, which is one of the oldest forms of storytelling, can still have an explosive impact on our lives. It aims to throw these stories, these small hand grenades of the heart, out into society to provoke personal revelations and revolutions. Slowly, each heart in turn, we can take down walls and welcome in each other because, where there is space for a story, there is space for a whole world.

With four concrete pillars marking out a large thrust performance space, an eclectic mix of audience seating on three sides of the stage, and a craft beer bar, The Bunker is a visceral and unique performance space with a character of its own.

The Bunker believes in artists. We give ambitious artists a home in which to share their work with adventurous audiences. We are champions of each piece that we programme and we want to ensure our stage is filled with exciting, exhilarating and contemporary theatre featuring artists that represent the world that we live in.

The Bunker was opened in October 2016 by founding directors Joshua McTaggart and Joel Fisher. The theatre's first year of work included the award-winning sell-out show *Skin a Cat*, Cardboard Citizen's 25th Anniversary epic *Home Truths*, and the world premiere of *31 Hours*. In-house productions have included *Abigail*, *Eyes Closed, Ears Covered* and *Devil With the Blue Dress*.

In September 2018, Artistic Director Chris Sonnex joined Executive Director David Ralf to lead the theatre's small but dedicated team, several of whom were involved in the original conversion of the space. Bunker Theatre Productions CIC is a not-for-profit theatre, which currently receives no public subsidy.

Find Out More

Website: www.bunkertheatre.com
Box Office: 0207 234 0486
E-Mail: info@bunkertheatre.com
Address: 53a Southwark Street, London, SE1 1RU

The Bunker Team

Artistic Director: Chris Sonnex
Executive Director: David Ralf
Head of Production: Hannah Roza Fisher
General Manager: Lee Whitelock
Front of House Manager: Ed Theakston

Boots

'Trees are poems that the earth writes upon the sky.'

Kahil Gibran, *Sand and Foam*

'A healthy tree is well-grounded because it has great roots.
You'll experience stormy days and blue-sky days,' she said,
'but your job as the tree isn't to grab the weather – it's to
experience the weather and let it pass.'

Shauna Niequist, *Present Over Perfect*

'Then one day, it's all over. The truck snaps and the tree's
life is at an end. "Finally", you can almost hear the young
trees-in-waiting sigh. In the years to come, they will quickly
push their way up past the crumbling remains. But service
in the forest doesn't end when life ends. The rotting cadaver
continues to play an important role in the ecosystem for
hundreds of years.'

Peter Wohlleben, *The Hidden Life of Trees*

'And all the lives we ever lived and all the lives to be are full
of trees and changing leaves.'

Virginia Woolf, *To the Lighthouse*

BOOTS

'Boots' is set in Boots, the chemist, in the village of Hurtmore, near Guildford and Salwester woods nearby. Centre stage is a bright white floor, payment counter and sets of shelves which are filled with varying products, all blank and all white. It is so 'sanitised' and pristine it is almost unreal. A shop sign hangs above, saying 'Boots'. Numbing, bland 'muzak' plays as the audience enter, including 'Ain't No Stoppin Us Now' by McFadden and Whitehead. Stage left and stage right are great trees, growing through a soil floor and between the sets of shelves where the aisles would be. They are so detailedly real they could almost be growing through the building. The trees on one side are from the Northern Hemisphere and the trees the other side are from the Southern Hemisphere, but they are all part of one forest. In the corner, apart from the other trees, is a Weeping Willow tree.

Notes on the text

(/) denotes interruption/next character speaking
(–) denotes a character lost for words/unresponsive

Scene One

Seeds

Willow, *a woman of colour, is serving a customer in Boots the chemist. She acts out the female customer.*

Willow   Can I help you?

A **Woman**, *she's got good vibes, 30ish, nice coat, good lapels, looks at me.*

Woman   'Yes, sorry I um just wondering if . . .'

'Well, I've got a really itchy um –'.

Beat.

'Yes, well, it's really bad, I can't sleep.'

Willow   Okay, what's itchy?

Woman   'My um'

She points vaguely to the bottom half of her body.

'My Front Area'

Willow   Your . . . front area?

Woman (*nods vigorously, whispers*)   'You know.'

Willow *frowns, still unclear.*

Woman (*whispers, emphatically*)   'My China!'

Willow   Oh, sorry, we don't do crockery.

Woman (*whispers*)   'My vagina.'

Willow (*to audience, really loudly*)   HER VAGINA.

(*Back to woman, compassionately.*) You've got thrush madam.

I keep a handle on myself, give her Canesten Duo, and she pays and leaves.

Willow *does an impression of the* **Woman** *walking off, trying not to itch. She comes back to audience and speaks.*

Lady bits? Lady bum? Front bottom?

She offers the words out to the audience almost as if they can pick which one is theirs.

Woo-woo? Noonee? Twinkle? Peach. Flower. Minko. Mimi. Yoni. Tilly. Mary. Aunty Mary. Froo-froo. Vajayjay. Fairy. Sugar Puff. Minnie. Mini ha ha. Froobuloo. Special Place.

Beat.

Really. / *Beat.* / What is wrong with VAGINA?

I reckon JK Rowling noticed it too. That's where she got everyone in her books not being able to say Voldemort from.

The Powerful Wizard Vagina!!

Whispered loudly.

She-Who-Must-Not-Be-Named!

Beat.

And don't even get me started on '*vulva*'!

Pause.

I've just moved here but 'china'?! That's got to be among my top ten. As a pharmacist you get to hear them all. And I mean *all*.

I can keep a straight face, but I still find it a beautiful moment.

She smiles kindly.

Scene Two

Germination

It's funny, this all started on a day I let a bit of my self-control go, you know?

I'm basically working two jobs to make ends meet right now so I got to work on little sleep and a lot of coffee.

Sleep deprivation can really mess with your head, but . . .
Need my space right now and, yeah, it doesn't come cheap.
But it's a new year, a new place and a new me!
I've even started doing pelvic floor exercises while I wait for Netflix to load.

She sinks back into the tiredness that engulfed her that day.

Anyway, don't think my 'Dickhead Alert' was fully switched on, when . . .

She jumps back in time to tell us the story, and acts out **Man** *herself.*

Man   'Alright love, yeah, my girlfriend's got something.'

Willow   Ah, oh, hello. Yes, okay. Is she able to come in herself?

Man   'Nah, nah.'

Willow   Okay, what are the symptoms? Perhaps I can help with something off the /

Man   'Yeah, basically. Seriously burning pee, and a lot, you know. Going for a slash, A LOT.'

Willow   Right, and your girlfriend, has she had this before?

Man   'Yeah loads, so boring innit, she's always on about it.'

Beat.

'So . . . so what do I need for that?'

Willow   Well it sounds like cystitis, if it's only mild some painkillers will help and lots of fluids to flush it out.

She picks up a packet of painkillers and puts them quietly on the counter.

Man   'Cool thanks love.'

Willow   If symptoms persist, I think your girlfriend may need to see a GP and get some antibiotics. A recurrent case could signal more significant problems.

Man   'Nahh, only significant problem is the lack of action, you know what I'm saying!'

Willow (*Out to the audience.*) That wasn't when I lost my control.

Man   'Yeah, while I'm here, I've got a bit of a pain in my hand.'

Willow   Is it muscular or /

Man   'Oh it's *all* muscle, love!'

Willow (*Out to the audience.*) No, still had that control.

Man   'It's here by my thumb, at the side, when I do this' (*she mimes the Tinder swipe action*). 'It's a bit swollen, very tender.

Pause.

'It can get very, very stiff.'

His thumb pops upwards like an erection.

Willow (*Out to the audience.*)   Still got it!

Willow (*back to* **Man**)   If it's RSI you may need a support for that or, perhaps, *give it a rest?*

Man   'Has anyone ever told you, you've got a very caring instinct? Very nurturing. I like that.'

Beat. He leans in towards **Willow**.

'I see that in you. I do. I'm not like other guys you know. I like your kind, you know, you're like, exotic. I like that, I really do. Seriously, what are you doing after work?'

Willow *looks out at audience, about to spit venom, swallows it and turns back to the* **Man** *with all her control on full blast.*

Willow   I'm here to help you with any issues that do not require a GP.

If there's anything you would like to know about the products we have on display, I can be of assistance.

Meanwhile, the cashier is on the left, right beside the *exit*.

Other than that, I am not interested.

(*Out to audience.*) Yes, I still held it!!

Man   'Oooo, cold man, ice! Okay, I get it, I get it, time of the month and all that. Guess I'll just take these and go. (*As he goes.*) Your loss, *Brown Sugar*, your loss . . .'

Willow *plays the* **Man** *walking out.*

She becomes herself in the scene with the **Man** *again.*

LOSS??!!
The only loss here is to the evolutionary gene pool,
that managed to let a racist,
sexist, lying,
trumped up,
dickhead like you through the net,
with a case of cystitis,
Tinder thumb RSI
and such a bad case of halitosis it could knock out a fucking army,
you ignorant
pond-life
FUCK-WIT!

Foresters have a name for it. 'Habitat Specific.'
It's when a plant can only grow in certain conditions in certain areas.
They can't adapt.
Take 'em out of their comfort zone and they die.
With climate change, those plants and trees are dying out.

That thought comforts me
I just think 'You're dying out.

The climate is changing and you're dying out. The internet, migration,
inter-racial marriage.
One day we'll all be like me,
one big mixed bag of genes from everywhere.
Race so mixed there won't be RACE any more.
And if you can't adapt to that climate,
your genes will
die
out.'

Enter **Liz**.

Liz   Christ!

Willow *freezes*.

Willow   I thought the shop was empty.

But I turned round and saw this old, white woman wearing a rain mac, tweed and muddy wellies, and thought 'Oh my god I'm fucked. She's going to tell my manager, he's going to put it on record . . . and here we go again, I'm fucked!'

She turns to look at **Liz**, *an older woman, frozen in the moment. She has a wheelie shopping basket, and is peering over the top of her glasses towards* **Willow** *and the* **Man**. *She's got a waterproof hair scarf on and has been rained on.*

Liz (*nods vaguely, turning a thought over in her head*)   Well, *I'd* have said too much fiddling on his computer games because he hasn't got any friends in real life,
but I guess that sort of thing's prehistoric.
You young people know all about this Tinder stuff, nowadays.

Looks towards where the **Man** *excited*.

Sad. Lonely people are just so unpleasantly desperate.
What a
cunt.

Suddenly there are peals of giggling laughter from the men's section. We can hear a group of girls spraying a can.

Willow   Er . . . sorry . . . I'll just be one minute!

She runs round to the aisle and stands with her hands on her hips.

Willow   Oi you lot, you spray for it, you pay for it! Now put that back or I'll start talking to you about Safe Sex again!

There are more peals of laughter, and whoops of joy as the girls go running out of the shop. **Willow** *comes back to* **Liz**.

Willow   Sorry about that.

Liz   Blimey. What was that?

Willow   Year 10s.

Liz   They're excited.

Willow (*looking at the girls, smiling*)   Yes, that's Lynx Africa for you. They sneak in, spray it all over themselves and discuss 'Dominic'.

Liz   Dominic?

Willow   Apparently they've all got off with him –

She stops – thinking that she's said too much.

Liz   Mmm, lucky Dominic.

Willow   If I don't catch them soon enough, they get to the condoms and start blowing them up.

Liz   Well, it's certainly all changed since my day. Only time I ever tried to buy a 'johnny', I got taken aside – in this very chemist, as it happens – and told it wasn't their policy and that I was a 'filthy little hussy'.

Liz *has walked round and put two items on the counter.*

Willow   Oh. I am sorry, that doesn't sound like much fun.

Liz   I have always wondered what my life could have been with more 'johnnies' in it. I could have been climbing mountains, kayaking rapids in Slovakia, abseiling the gherkin. Who knows! Certainly not buying incontinence pads in Hurtmore village chemist.

Willow   Oh, did you know it's three for two on Tena Lady Discreets?

Liz   I did yes, but I don't need three, I only need two.

Willow   Okay. Would you be interested in Nivea's New Passion Fruit Body Lotion, it's on offer madam?

Liz   Nope, I'm sure I've had more passion that Nivea's had new fruit, whoever's offering!

Willow (*laughs, despite herself*)   Okay, that's four pound ninety eight.

Liz *starts looking in the big bag for her purse, she puts her head right in.*

Willow   Do you have an advantage card?

Liz   No, I've never found anything advantageous about them.

(*Head still in the bag, casually.*) I've got to go, I've left Jeremy in the utility room.

Willow   Oh, your dog?

Liz   No, my husband, unfortunately.

Willow (*laughing*)   Oh! . . . how would you like to pay, cash or card?

Liz (*She pops her head out of the bag holding her purse, triumphant.*)   Cash!

Willow   Do you know if you spend over five pounds you can get a ten pound Number 7 Anti Ageing Cosmetics Voucher, you'd need to use before the 31st of this month. Is that something that would interest you?

Liz   I'd rather make a pavlova out of my own eyeballs.

Willow (*again, laughing*)   Right. I hear you.

She gives **Liz** *the Tena Lady.*

So that's two pence change.

Liz   Thank you.

(*Gesturing to the* **Man.**) And well done.

Liz *starts to leave.*

Willow   Thank you.

Liz   Vive La Revolution!

Exit **Liz.**

Willow (*To audience.*)   I like her.

Scene Three

Photosynthesising.

Liz *is walking in the woods, after shopping and meeting* **Willow** *for the first time. She addresses the audience and trees.*

Liz   I usually walk most days.

Through the woods, to the shops, and then back again. Stop for a rest on this good old dead stump and –

She sits down on a dead tree. She pulls out a packet of fags and a small packet of matches. She holds the cigarettes as she speaks. She lights a match and watches the flame for a bit over the following speech. She doesn't light the cigarette, she's trying to give up.

Used to come with Dirk
Bogarde,
My dog.
But he died of course.
I say that phrase too much.
Lots of dogs and people.
Dying.

Since I've stopped working,
I've had a lot more 'me' time.
Which is quite shite really.
Retirement. I fucking hate that word.
'Retiiiiire.' Sounds like a yawn.
I am 'anti-tiring'.
I'm not remotely tired.
I sleep very well.

I think it's always annoyed Jeremy how well I sleep,
He likes to lie awake and listen to the World Service.
Used to drive me mad.
but then I discovered ear plugs, a silk eye mask,
and gin.

I got him dressed this morning, as usual.
Laid out his cable knit cardigan.
Golfing attire really, but he insists on wearing it still. Idiot.
Put his socks on his little skinny feet.
And he said he wasn't sure how he could keep going.

Pause.

I – I –
Told him the only way to survive is to be practical, to keep
doing things.
So, I wheeled him into the utility room and told him to sort
out the Tupperware cupboard.

Pause.

He's still there, I ought to get going, really.

Beat.

I stood in the doorway and watched him for a while and
thought how amazing it was that we once used to have sex.
That we made Oscar.
The world, everything, has changed so radically,
It's –
You think I'm going to start moaning about young people
being on their phones.

But I'm not.
Christ,
if we'd had Tinder and Snapchat things would have been far
more exciting.
We had to wait for Royal Mail to get their act together.
Imagine that.
Royal Mail and then the occasional chance frisson.
There is a lot to be said for anticipation though. Waiting
makes you savour it.
Do people do that, nowadays? Savour it?

Five years ago
I had a roll around with one of Jeremy's carers in the
conservatory.
Terribly sensitive soul.
He was an actor too, he had a very big part.

Beat.

Something at the National?
He said I reminded him of Helen Mirren –
it was lovely, slow, and very different from what I thought
youthful sex would be . . .

You know, women with their mouth half open,
looking like they are about to fall off their seat.
They never have a spine that works.
And men with the extra large watches.
Those ones that tell the time of every continent
and how many steps you've done that day.
Too many numbers,
not enough romance,
and too much emphasis on the wrist.

She does a wanking gesture.

I'm not sure about it all,
It always looks violent and very cold.

I do miss that cosiness and warmth.
I loved it,

I mean
having sex,
with nice people,
but now

I just don't know.
It seems fruitless.

She is gazing at the trees.

So, now in the early mornings,
instead of (*beat*) anything with Jeremy,
I walk.
In the woods.
Sometimes I even have a cigarette, the occasional one.
Or four.
And yes, I *know*, awful for you, but I've got to die of
something.

*Stares at cigarette she's playing with, she may even light it as she
speaks the next words, inhales.*

Is that all there is?

*Her mind has been somewhere else but she brings herself back to
the trees.*

I walk.
Through the big trees.
And see
the sunlight come flittering through,
I love it.
Takes my mind away from everything else.
Their strength and power.
And their differences.
Different personalities.
Of all the trees.
My father planted some of these.
The younger ones.
But some of these majestics live up to 300 years. Incredible.

If I was a tree, my life would have hardly begun.
So much yet to come. Only childhood behind me.

I started walking when I first got pregnant.
It helped the morning sickness.
I'd walk here, in the trees, vomit in the bushes if it was really bad,
But feel . . . better.
That was with my first pregnancy.
Second one not so much actual vomit,
just the constant feeling.

But walking here, every day, through these woods,
it was the only time I ever felt

Free.

Scene Four

Sprouting.

Willow *is counting out pills to make up prescriptions.*

Willow   That's the third prescription I've filled out for Obecalp since I've been here. (*She shakes her head, disillusioned.*) I've heard some patients swear it's a wonder drug and keep coming back for repeat prescriptions, but I don't know.

She is frustrated, angry even.

If it *is* all in the mind, and half of the symptoms are psychosomatic, then surely we should be treating the mind and the body as a whole?

Reflects.

I always wanted to be a pharmacist because I thought it would give me the chance to do patient care, but in reality I spend more time counting out pills than I do talking to people. I never thought it would be this . . . (*she looks around*) alone. (*She resigns herself to the moment and returns to her work.*)

She looks up as if someone has asked a question.

Obecalp?

Pause.

Placebo, spelt backwards.

She lets that register with the audience.

Oh yeah, and they come in different colours and sizes. The white or cream coloured ones are considered 'mild', red ones are meant to be the strongest because of their strong colour and size, and the black ones are only used *very* rarely. Patients report adverse 'side effects' from the black ones.

In reality, they're just a sugar pill. Yep, I might as well be handing out M&Ms (*she tosses one in her mouth*).

Liz *has materialised at her elbow.*

Liz   Where do you keep your Tampax then?

Willow *nearly chokes on the sugar pill and has to have a bang on the back from* **Liz** *in the process of the ensuing coughing fit.* **Liz** *wallops her with unrestrained fervour.*

Willow   Thanks, thanks! I'm alright now.

Liz   Jolly good. So, Tampax?

Willow   Er . . .

Liz   Cheapest brand please, none of this fragranced rubbish they make nowadays. Who wants their whistle smelling of the potpourri in a cheap hotel lobby, I really don't know.

Willow   Right, okay, yes, it's just over here.

Liz   Good, good.

As **Willow** *shows* **Liz** *to the products,* **Liz** *walks slightly ahead. Behind her / aside,* **Willow** *says to the audience 'Whistle? Brilliant'.*

Willow   Are they for you . . . ?

Liz Christ, no! They're for Jeremy. (**Willow** *looks even more taken aback*.) For his mouth. His breath smells like Ghandi's jockstrap at the moment, but it's nothing a good floss won't sort out.

Willow Right.

Liz I use 'em to wedge open his lip so I can get right to the back. Can't trust those dental roll things, nearly lost one down his throat once. But these have the handy little string on them which means I can yank the blighters back if everything starts to go south.

Willow Oh, you know, there are some great natural remedies for halitosis. Chlorophyll in plants is a powerful natural deodorizer – so if he chews something green like parsley or basil or even rosemary?

Liz Gosh, really? Is that what they're teaching in Boots nowadays? Alternative remedies?

Willow Oh no. No, definitely not!

Slight pause. **Liz** *is listening.*

That was from my research.

Liz *waits for her to go on and* **Willow** *risks sharing a bit more.*

I'm looking into the healing properties of plants.

Liz How fascinating.

Liz *is genuinely interested.*

Willow Yep, kinda keeps me awake at night but caffeine is a helpful, naturally occurring drug! Plants actually use it like an insecticide to deter pests. Oh, yes, and that's a good one too: green tea. The chlorophyll in green tea. For breath issues.

Liz If only. Sadly Jeremy's palate is distinctly 'British'. By which I mean decidedly closeted. Island mentality, I reckon. He's prepared to traverse the heady heights of shepherd's pie all the way to the soft shores of cauliflower cheese. But no further! If it's bland and stodgy he'll eat it. If it isn't, he has a toddler tantrum. Even gets upset if the Spotted Dick, I prostrate myself in making him, has got too many raisins in it.

Willow   Tricky customer.

Liz   Parkinson's. It's a bastard but what can you do?

Willow   Ah, I'm sorry. That must be hard. On both of you.

Liz   Well no one wants to feed Spotted Dick in one end only to watch it come out the other, do they. But anyway we cope. At least, we did. Hmmm. (*She thinks to herself.*)

Willow (*carefully*)   Do you have some support yourself?

Liz (*avoids the issue*)   Well, I've just changed to a wonderful new brand of support tights, if that's what you mean. Look!

She holds up her skirts and shows off her tights.

They even do them in patterns – aren't they lovely? Keep the varicose veins IN, the blood pumping ROUND and the knicker elastic UP!

She tap dances a few steps to show off her tights.

Now I'm ditching the car and with all these walks again, I'll be a new woman!

She has tap danced all the way over to her trolley.

Right, must dash!

Liz *exits with a flourish wheeling her shopping trolley behind her.*

Willow   Wow.

Every time I meet this lady it's just . . . I mean . . .

WOW.

She smiles.

Parkinson's though . . . that's really tough.

I don't – I couldn't – Not *that* kind of patient care. I wouldn't be able to do that.

Pause.

But . . .

'Get stuck in, Willow! You're wound up tight, holding everything back. It's no good. Get stuck in, eh!'

My old manager said that to me. Before I moved here. She was nice.

Before all the –

Pause.

Then it was all 'company protocol' and 'my hands are tied', 'there's nothing I can do . . .'

Beat.

and then 'We regret to inform you . . .' It's been . . . playing on my mind.

She holds up one of the 'Obecalp' pills she's been making up the prescription with.

'No Roots' by Alice Merton begins to play over the store sound system.

Willow *is moving around the store, restocking shelves, but slowly picks up the beat. She begins to be swept away by the song, dancing round the shop, stomping and whirling. She is hurt, angry and defiant but free and untethered, shaking it off, jumping up the kick step and off the shop counter. Towards the end of the song,* **Liz,** *in contrast, moves through the woods exhausted and emotional. She is holding a yellow A4 notice in her hand and checking each huge tree trunk for more, finding them and ripping them off angrily and discarding them. Finally they come abruptly to a stop, face to face, centre stage, unaware of each other's previous actions while the song has played.*

Scene Five

Shading.

Liz *is distracted and almost disorientated. Her clothes are unusually unkempt with splatters of mud, caught twigs and bits of bracken.*

Liz Er, hello dear, I need a few things, could I have some of those eye drops for an infection, he's got something stuck at the back. And I've got a prescription to pick up too.

She hands over the prescription and **Willow** *walks towards the counter.*

Willow For you right?

Liz *is clearly agitated, and struggling to focus, looking around the shop, her eyes resting nowhere.*

Liz What?

Willow Are they for you?

Liz (*snappy*) Of course they are.

Willow *is behind the counter. She looks at the prescription and then to audience.*

Willow It was for sleeping tablets and sertraline, the antidepressant. I suddenly felt worried about her.

I mean when you get to that age you should be sleeping properly and happy, right? You should be nodding off and dreaming about the Peak District. Right?

Willow (*to* **Liz**) You need to make sure you take the sertraline at the same time each day, it's usually best to take it first thing if you can.

Liz Alright.

Willow And the sleeping pills are strong, so you must only take one.

Liz I'll do as the doctor tells me, thank you.

Willow Okay, that is what the doctor suggests too.

Liz Fine, so I don't need to be told twice. Especially by the shop girl.

Willow (*to audience*) Oh right, yeah, here we go.

Willow (*back to* **Liz**)   I'm a qualified pharmacist, actually.

Liz   Really?

Willow   Yes.

Liz   You don't look like a qualified pharmacist.

Willow (*looks to the audience and then back to* **Liz**)   I'm not sure how to respond to that, I am, and this is my job while I also write for a scientific journal.

Liz   Scientific journal?

Willow   Yes.

Liz   Well, you don't look like a scientist either.

Pause as **Willow** *holds her self-control and decides how to respond. She is clearly hurt and shakes her head a little. She begins to turn away to retrieve the prescription, when:*

Willow (*she turns back to* **Liz**, *with a slither of ice in her voice*) Um, excuse me, actually, can I just ask. What do you think a scientist looks like?

Liz   I beg your pardon?

Willow   I just wondered.

Liz   What?

Willow   What your picture of a scientist actually is.

Liz   What are you talking about?

Willow   When you picture a scientist. What do you see?

Liz   I have no idea *what* you are talking about!

Willow   Or a pharmacist for that matter.

Liz   What?!

Willow   What does a pharmacist 'look' like?

Liz   Listen, young lady, I have no idea what you think you are talking about but I really don't have time for this!

Willow   You don't have time for this?

Liz   No, I do not!

Willow   This is literally 'beneath your time'?

Liz   I have just found these god awful notices.

She holds out the notices.

Willow   It's actually not worthy of your actual time?

Liz   Proposing to cut down my /

Willow   It's not actually worth your precious attention?

Liz   Listen, I don't know what is wrong with you, but I /

Willow   I'm sorry, what? I'm 'wrong', am I? Just how exactly am I 'wrong', eh? What is it about me that you find quite so *wrong*?!

Liz   PLEASE! For god's sake! Just stop! Just *stop!* Just give me my prescription and I'll go!

Pause. **Willow** *puts the prescription on the countertop.* **Liz** *is almost in tears. She leaves the yellow, laminated notice on the counter and shoves the prescription in her bag.* **Liz** *begins to leave.*

Willow   Okay, look, I'm sorry if I lost my temper but perhaps you don't understand that /

Willow *tries to follow* **Liz**.

Liz   What I *understand*, young woman, is that I will be speaking to your manager! This is absolutely unacceptable –

Willow   Um, hang on, / listen,

Liz   No, it is! It is entirely unacceptable to harass / an old lady like me

Willow   No, I was trying to /

Liz   On a day like this!

Willow   Okay I think you need to / hear me out

Liz   When I've just discovered those blood suckers are after my woods, and everything!

Willow   What I was / trying to say was

Liz   I just can't believe it! I didn't think this day could get any worse! But apparently, it *can*.

Willow   No, that's not /

Liz   I will be *speaking* to your manager!

Exit **Liz**. **Willow** *is left in the shop, alone. Pause. She sinks to the floor.*

Willow   Oh my god, oh my *god* Willow! What . . . What are you doing?!

This is not – Fuck . . .

Oh my god and now my manager and . . . Oh, fuck.

I can't move again. If I lose my job again, if I . . . Oh god!

What was I thinking?!

'Don't let 'em see it get to you!'

'Keep your head held high and don't let 'em see it get to you.'

She gets up, drained, trying to 'resolutely' return to her work. But she can't.

But, oh fuck, I don't know who I'm fighting any more! Am I fighting them and picking up on every crappy little comment that comes out of their idiotic mouths or . . . or . . . am I fighting myself? Telling myself to 'rise above it', 'let it go', 'forget about it', 'get on with my life'? Shove your feelings down and don't get angry, don't show it hurts, don't . . .

Pause.

How many fights do I have to fight? Where does it end? Can't hold it back, can't let it go.

What am I supposed to do?

I can't . . .

Keep on fighting like this. (*Pause.*) But then . . .

Starting a row with a narrow-minded, sheltered old woman in a chemist in Surrey is hardly *The Revolution* is it?

Scene Six

Hibernation.

Willow   When I – When I lose my . . . When it goes . . . my self-control . . .

Boots disappears and **Willow** *turns suddenly to find herself standing on the edge of the forest.*

I'm back there again.

The trees are lit in reds and greens, long shadows. Dark and foreboding.

Standing on the edge of the wood.

Looking in.
Watching in.
Shut out.
The Outsider.

The trees are all growing, blossoming, stretching up, nurtured by the light, enjoying the sunshine.

The light on the trees has changed, it is light and beautiful.

They are beautiful. Healthy. 'Insiders.'

But I'm not.

Now **Willow** *is the one casting a long shadow, cold and alone.*

I'm not one of them.
I'm on my own.

And the soil under my feet is teaming, rippling, bristling
with life.
And I dig my hands in deep
To be part of it.

Willow *sinks her hands into the soil.*

Rich earth,
Humus,
Topsoil,
Eluviation,
Subsoil,
Regolith,
Bedrock.

And I want to know
What's in each layer

She digs.

What nurtures the trees, what makes them unfurl
Into the healthy ones.
How does it work, how do they grow?

Water, food, shelter, yes, yes, they have all that
But . . .
what else?

She is up to her elbows in soil.

And then my hands meet
Something soft
Stringy and fibrous
Tendrils and subsystems

She smiles.

The Mycorrhizal Network.

The 'Wood Wide Web'.
The hidden connection.

She gets excited.

Miles and miles of fungi

She has dug her hands in deep and her arms and face are smeared in soil.

Between the roots
As big as whole regions!
Or as small as local plant systems
Working with the trees
Connecting the forest.
Exchanging water, carbon, nitrogen, phosphorus, defence compounds, allelochemicals, it just doesn't stop!
Beech to chestnut, alder to elm, sycamore to oak, hawthorn to holly, maple to pine! Communicating, talking.
It's all there!
Warning the pest attacks and the water shortages.
Everyone pitching in
Sharing the messages, sharing the resources,
Moving the carbon, exchanging the nutrients
Plant to plant, tree to tree,
Living being to Living being.
No one is left out
Everything is shared.
Everything is *fair*.

Pause.

Even the willow.

She turns. She smiles at the tree in the corner. The willow tree.

The Pioneer.
Tiny light seeds, easily carried on the wind
So they can strike out on their own, open up new habitats.
A 'pioneer species'.

Standing alone from the forest,
Breaking new ground
But still connected

She plunges her hands into the soil again.

through its roots.

She smiles.

As she speaks the next section she is digging out and following the mycorrhizal fungi, like a string underground from the forest towards the Willow.

Sometimes called the 'Hollow Willow'
Because it stands alone.
A tree that people could steal off to, and tell their secrets,
Without fear of being overheard . . .

I sometimes feel like that.
As pharmacist,
The 'Keeper of the Secrets'.
All the whispered problems,
Private fears and shames
Spoken through the body's ill health.
Swimming round and round in your head
by the end of the day.
Everyone desperate for redemption.

She is sadder.

Everyone desperate for . . . absolution.

Got too much and . . .

The panic attacks started.
Got worse.
Didn't know when one was coming.
Couldn't see straight, took over.
Took time, took money, and finally . . .
Took my job. Had to move again.

She suddenly leaves digging up the Mycorrhizal trail, to walk around the trees.

Came out here. To the Burbs.
Did you know you have better mental health if you live on a street with trees?
Yep, better surrounding habitat, birds, insects, trees

You're more likely to walk, exercise, live longer
Better life expectancy of seven years.

Seven years! That's a lot.

Willow trees only have an average life of 50 years.
If they're lucky, 70.
Pioneer species. Out there on their own, see.
Grow fast, grow hard, but don't save their energy.
That's not going to be me.
I'm not going away easy, no siree! Not me.
So come out here to live better and live *longer*.

She smiles.

Healthy roots, healthy canopy,
Just like this beauty.

She has walked back to the Willow tree.

How are you doing?

She puts a hand on the tree.

What's your story? Have you come far?
I wonder where you're from? Let's have a look.

She digs among the roots.

Why is this . . .
Where's your mycorrhizal connec –
What is this?

She brings up her hands covered in stinking rot.

It's rotted.
How can it be . . .
Why are you . . . How can . . .

She looks around, seeing the unnatural lighting and intangible setting. **Willow** *begins to realise she's in the lost time of one of her panic attacks.*

No!
It can't be!

No! No!
Not again!

She cries.

Please don't be rotted! Please, please, not again! Please, no!

She begins to dig frantically.

SFX (*whispers reverberate around the stage from different corners*)

Shame, shame, disgusting, filthy, dirty.
Shame.
Unwashed. Unclean.
Shame.
Unwanted.

SHAME.

The sounds torture **Willow***, she backs away, terrified, covering her ears.*

No! No! Stop! Stop!
Make it stop!!

She flees.

Exit **Willow***.*

Scene Seven

Saplings.

Liz *is walking in the wood, she's very tearful. Same day.*

I don't think I've felt this tearful in thirty years.
It's best to cry when walking.
Gets it out quicker.
And no one has to see it.

Today, the shop, the notices, and . . .
I just . . .

A good cry can make you feel so much better, can't it?
I read a wonderful fact once, about crying. It was in the
colour supplement of the *Telegraph*.
Apparently there's a high concentration of the stress
hormone, cortisol, in tears.
So crying really does help you to calm down because it
flushes out the toxins that are all swirling round your head
at the time.

Bloodsucking bastards. How dare they try and take my
trees?
Slapping notices on them, willy nilly, making way for
'redevelopment'
Like they don't matter! It's a crime! Council Criminals, that's
what they are. Not Town Planning. Environment
Eviscerating, more like.
If they take a whole wood!? Should be done for bloody
genocide or whatever it is!

*She's very tearful, goes to light a cigarette but the matches are soggy
and won't burn.*

FUCK! Of-bloody-course.

She throws them away in frustration.

*She sighs and gets out her vape instead, turns it on and starts
inhaling.*

Oscar bought me this for Mother's Day. Peach Cream flavour
juice. One of my signature puddings, very thoughtful of
him.

Except this doesn't have any Cointreau *or* nicotine in it, so
it's basically totally fucking pointless.

*She looks at it in disgust, but then habit kicks in and she puffs on it
again.*

'Is that all there is?'

*She hums a few bars of Peggy Lee's 'Is That all there is?'. She vapes
a bit more.*

I need these trees. We all need these trees
They make up the community
They are the community.
Fuck, bloody Hurtmore village hasn't got much going for it
But at least it's got Salwester Woods.
I *need* them, I . . .
Where do I go without them?

(*Pause.*)

They just called it the baby blues in those days, but I knew it
was more than that. Jeremy refused to come to the hospital,
but I *insisted* the nurses let me hold him. All blue.
Swollen and not moving.

(*Pause.*)

So I came here. Here was the only place I found some . . .
Something. To hold on to.

(*Pause.*)

And then I got pregnant again so soon after. (*Beat.*) Oscar.
Oscar moved and wriggled and screamed and cried.

And cried

And cried

And the crying never seemed to stop.
Torture.
Sleep deprivation, screaming,
crying torture.
I would find myself holding his little head near the kitchen
counter top, thinking how easily I could smash it in.
I only held on by putting him at the end of the garden in his
pram until the screaming stopped. And then I would rush
out, terrified I'd be there holding another blue, cold baby
again.

But I wasn't.
He was asleep.
It was okay.

The panic would dissipate a little, until it washed back down into empty numbness.

Pause. She takes a deep breath.

Even then, Jeremy wanted more children.
He came from a large family and just seemed to take it for granted that he'd have lots of children himself.
Never asked how I imagined the future.

I just knew I couldn't.
I was lost at sea and barely keeping myself from drowning,
Holding on by my fingernails, taking my daily walk here.
And the one thing I could see was the Lighthouse that was The Pill.
Godsend.
Wonderful, wonderful, miracle, godsend!

Took it for years before he found out.

He'd go on about us 'just not being lucky' and saying he was sure it would happen for us in the end.
All those god-awful patronising, meaningless shit that people come out with and I'd whimper and smile and nod and hold the secret of my salvation deep inside.

Terrible, the night that he found out. (It was) Never the same again.

She smokes.

Scene Eight

Blight.

Willow *is at work on high alert.*

Willow   I played days of cat and mouse after that.
Swapping shifts, looking over my shoulder,
Ducking down beneath the shelves of Wind-eze and Alcazeltzer,
Trying not to let one go myself.

Leaving and entering every day by the back door
To avoid the

She mimes a tap on the shoulder.

I couldn't bear the thought.
Not again.

She grabs her coat and bag, and is leaving from a day's work.

But then,
One day

She is arriving again.

There was a protest

She tries to enter the shop by the back door, but can't.

Blocking the road behind the shop
So I had to come in the front

Willow *enters by the front door, closes the door behind her but looks back through the glass window to try to see what the protest is about.*

And I wondered what it was about.
Pensioners. On mobility scooters.
With placards.

She strains her eyes to read them.

'We won't stand for it!'
'Because some of us can't stand!
'But we won't sit for it, either!'

She is trying to make sense of that, when.

And then

She is suddenly stiff, frozen. She feels the tap tap tap on her shoulder.

She turns slowly, the dread rising.

My manager.

Manager   I've been looking for you.

Willow   I – I –

Manager   I think you need to see this.

Manager *hands* **Willow** *a piece of paper.* **Willow** *holds it, shaking and slowly lowers her eyes to read it.*

Willow   Oh.

Pause.

Oh!

Pause.

OH!

She is flooded with relief, tears pricking her eyes.

Willow   I mean, yes! Er, um, thank you! That's . . . er, once it's built it, that'd be . . . brilliant. Thank you!

Manager *has walked off.* **Willow** *calls after them.*

Thank you!

Willow *is looking down at the paper, reading it again, absorbing its contents when* **Liz** *arrives suddenly behind her.*

Liz   I can't find Vaseline.

Willow (*she turns*)   It's next to lip balms.

By the end of the sentence she's recognised who it is.

Oh.

Liz   Yes, I know, but I don't want those ridiculous small pots, I need a big tub with a proper lid.

Willow   –

Liz   It's for my curtain poles.

Willow   Your curtain poles?

Liz   Yes they need lubrication, the rings get stuck and make this terribly unpleasant grating sound –

Willow   Right.

Liz   It's driving Jeremy round the bend, and I can't change them because I've just spent thousands on getting matching pelmets.

Willow   –

Liz   Pelmets, like a helmet for the curtain pole?

Willow   –

Liz   Pelmets cover up the curtain poles, such ugly things, (**Willow** *looks blank*) Christ, what do they teach nowadays? Mine are from Laura Ashley. Quintessentially British. Well, used to be, it's now owned by some bloody company in Malaysia. I mean, honestly. Least we've still got good old Boots, eh?

Willow   Um – Boots was actually bought by a private equity firm in Switzerland. In 2007.

Liz   Godfathers! Really? Are you . . . ? – well that's the Swiss for you, only good for chocolate, cheese and so much money they don't know what to do with it. Except go round buying up other people's chemists, evidently.

Pause. **Willow** *says nothing. She takes an inbreath to say something to break the tension, when.*

'Think of what our Nation stands for,
Books from Boots and country lanes,
Free speech, free passes, class distinction,
Democracy and proper drains'

Willow *is appalled but* **Liz** *looks quite pleased with herself for remembering it, at least.*

Had to learn that at school. Some class competition or something. Couldn't remember it at the time, got a right ticking off, and now can't get the bloody thing out of my brain, of course. It's all rubbish but we weren't taught to question it. Just repeat it. That's all.

Pause.

I've been thinking about that lately. From what you said.

Willow   I'm sorry?

Liz   Yes. From what you said.

Willow *begins to look over her shoulder, fearful this is actually the 'tap on the shoulder'.*

Willow   From what I said?

Liz   You said 'what does a pharmacist or a scientist look like?'

Willow   Look, if this is about /

Liz   And you were right.

Willow   What?

Liz   In my day they looked like that spiteful old git who gave me a dressing down in here and called me names. And I wasn't taught to question him. I wasn't taught to stand up and turn round and question the status quo.

Willow   So . . . ?

Liz   And that's good.

Willow *still looks blank.*

That you did that. That you do that.

Pause. The two women look at each other.

Liz   Women are taught to be obedient. Not to raise objections.

Willow (*cautiously*)   We can't have that any more.

Liz   No.

Willow   That works for . . . a few people, but not for . . . everyone else.

Liz   Very true. Very . . . unfair.

Pause. The two women look at each other.

Liz (*she smiles*)   Anyway, do you have any proper tubs of Vaseline for my poles?

Willow   We might do in the infant section, usually people buy it for –

Liz   Of course –

Willow/Liz   Nappy rash.

They both smile at each other and **Willow** *points in the direction of Vaseline,* **Liz** *goes to get it, talking as she does.*

Liz   My son Oscar used to have terrible nappy rash, painful red blotches of over his little arse . . . I used to lather him in vaseline, like a slippery eel. He's an art dealer now. Fifty fucking four. It's quite good for lots of things really, chapped lips, squeaky door knobs, curtain poles, of course we always used it for well a good old /

Willow   Yep, er many uses, and is there anything else you need?

Liz   No, that's it. Do you have children?

Willow (*a bit taken aback*)   Um, no, I don't.

Liz   Why?

Willow   Um – I um well, I don't have a boyfriend for a start.

Liz   Well you should. How old are you?

Willow   Um. (*She almost doesn't answer.*) I'm thirty-five.

Liz   Jesus Fucking Christ. Thirty-five? What are you doing? We've got to get you out there, my girl! Oscar's PA is delicious. I shall tell him to come in and say hello.

Willow   I'm alright actually, but thanks.

Liz   No, darling, you are not alright. We've got to get you moving. When Oscar was born, it was just everything.

Willow (*annoyance is really rising*)   I um – really – is there anything else you need?

Liz   But honestly, having children is completion for a woman – at least, that's what they say!

Willow   I can't have children.

Liz   Of course you can darling, I'll send Nathanial in. He's divine.

Willow   No, I mean, I can't have children, I um –

She decides whether she's going to say it and then just does.

have blocked fallopian tubes. I can't conceive.

Liz   Oh – gosh – right.

Pause. She doesn't know what to say.

Have you tried a white wine vinegar douche? My godmother used to swear by that /

Willow   It's really a rather personal issue if that's OK.

She's actually quite upset but trying to conceal it.

Liz   Oh god! There I go again, putting my foot in it, just when we were –

Willow   Can I help you with anything else?

Liz   No, just the Vaseline, thank you. Oh and yes, another prescription for more of these glorious sleeping tablets.

Willow (*to audience*)   I sorted the prescription for her – I just wanted her to go – but, as she walked past the painkillers, she picked up two packets of Nurofen Express and shoved them in her bag.

She nicked them.

I couldn't believe it.
I've seen kleptomaniacs at work before but . . .
Her? A shoplifter. *For real?* I can't believe –

And all that telling me to have kids . . .
It's bullshit, I don't have to do *anything*!

Pause.

I just.

She is reeling.

It was . . . she said . . . I think . . .

Longer pause.

And then I can feel the darkness rising again
Like a cloud of smoke and fumes cloying my brain.

The lights change reverting to the states of Scene Six. **Willow**
pivots.

And I'm back there again
Back in the woods and

She screams.

NO!

Blackout.

Scene Nine

Snagging.

Liz *is sitting in the woods. She vapes.*

Liz   I suppose I shouldn't have come out with that crap
about kids to the girl in the chemist, but it's just what you
say, isn't it? And she had that face on her, like she wanted
them so badly.

She reflects.

She knows so little, poor darling.

Pause.

Now that I think of it, Jeremy always went silent himself
when we were younger and our friends had a new baby and
finally, he wouldn't visit them with me.
Wouldn't even talk about it.

I see it now. The sadness in him. He'd been going on and on
about wanting to be with 'Oscar and the baby' and I finally
broke and shouted, 'What are you on about, you useless old
moron! Oscar hasn't got a baby!'

And he just said 'No. The first one'.

Pause.

Now, what do I do with that? We'd never talked about it for
all these years but there suddenly was the emptiness and the
hurt and the pain, lying out – raw – between us, like he only
died yesterday.

Pause.

Stupid really,
marriage at 19,
but there wasn't any other option in those days.
And the ridiculous thing was, I thought it WAS freedom!
I thought it was adulthood and having a say in things and
being established and respected.
No longer being the naive young girl in pink tights and red
boots who fell pregnant in the woods behind the cricket
pavilion.

That was the fork in the road that day.
A silly bet with my friend Sarah
She didn't believe I'd do it.
But I bowled in there, all falsies and front
And said
'I'll take one packet of prophylactics to go, please!'

Pause.

I'd seen it on an American TV show.
Thought it'd sound better if I used a fancy word.

Silence was more deafening than a Trappist Monk's funeral.

She smokes.

I won the bet but lost . . .
My future.
Didn't know the sickness was coming.
The vomiting and then the rot that never left.

Finally it came down to one hope.
I believed that it would go, when he did.
When Jeremy died, I would revel in the freedom again.
I'd burn up the floor as I danced out all the fire in me again!

She does a few small dance steps but, she tires and they peter out too quickly.

But now I wonder that it isn't so much a part of me,
that I have built myself around it.
Am I just a shell?
A vessel for this rotting, stinking blackness inside me, that
seeps out in droplets of poison all around?

I don't know if that's life, really, is it?
Is there any point to being alive, if that's it?
Why can't I kill it?
Why won't it go?

Scene transition – Peggy Lee – 'Is That All There Is?' (verse about the circus)

Scene Ten

Flowering.

(Two days later. A Friday. Willow is yawning after a late night writing and waking up very slowly. She is re-stocking shelves and adding tags to the prices.)

Willow (*she puts a box on the shelf*)   Buy One Get One Free
Imodium? Bargain.
Nothing like 241 Week to bring you back down to earth.

She yawns.

Sold nine morning after pills this morning.

She nods quietly and thinks about it, slightly sad.

They're not on offer but it's quite normal for a Friday morning.
Lots of people get smashed on a Thursday night, and find themselves struggling to make eye-contact with a pharmacist the next morning.

I've done – (that)
I mean, we've all – (done that)
Didn't know it was pointless until a year ago.

Long pause.

We pharmacists get to see so much shame.
There was this one lady,
about 40,
who came in for a loofah and KY Jelly for her 'sister's cat' or something.
She was mortified and practically tried to tell me the cat's entire life story to prove it was real.
I nodded and listened
and nodded
and listened
but what I was really thinking was:
'Love. I hope you have THE most fun you've ever had with that KY Jelly. And then I hope you learn to order it online, and in **bulk** for your future.'

Suddenly she's snapped wide awake.

And then suddenly my Sunday Morning Runner is in and I haven't noticed him until he's at my elbow. I've seen him a few times and thought (*her face makes an appreciative look*) but now he's asking my advice about athlete's foot and I'm trying to sound sensible and focused, whilst thinking how clingy that sweaty t-shirt is.

He's twinkly and present and it's like we were just knocking up some scrambled eggs together rather than discussing his peeling, rotting trench-foot.

And now it's me that's sweaty.

'Is there anything else I could help you with?' I said, whilst thinking 'like taking your clothes off', and he asked for 'just deodorant, please.' I showed him and he said 'Oh yes, of course, the one and only *men's* aisle. As if men only need 10% correction, but women have to have 90% of the stuff in here aimed at them. It's ridiculous really'.

Pause.

I've never actually orgasmed at work, but this was as close as I came.

She walks like the woman in Scene One who had thrush.

The walk to the tills afterwards was like I was the Christmas Tree and he'd just turned the fairy lights on.

But then I saw Liz, out of the corner of my eye, charging down the shop towards me.

Mr Athlete's Foot was last in the queue and I can feel his eyes on me while I serve the bloke buying Dulcolax and Deep Heat and then an itching mum lucking out on 241 Head Lice Shampoo. Finally it's his turn and his fingers brush mine as he hands over the antifungal cream, while my eyes wander up his body to find his (eyes). When /

Liz   Sorry. Shouldn't have said it. Didn't mean it. Hope you weren't offended.

Willow (*caught off guard*)   Err, sorry, what?

Liz   Yes. We shouldn't perpetuate the bullshit and I've thought long and hard about it, and that was what I was doing.

Willow (*surprised/incredulous/confused*)   The bullshit? I could see the expression on Mr Athlete's Foot change.

Liz   Oh come on! That crap about children completing us. It's not true, no one questions it and I wished I had lamped the first woman who said it to me.

Willow   Mr Athlete's Foot is looking round, searching for a way out.

Liz   Just because you've got a womb doesn't mean you should be forced to use it. And some women are just really not cut out for childcare. I find myself really rather cross with the whole Virgin Mary, self-sacrificing, doormat-to-motherhood bullshit.

Willow (*panicking*)   Mr Athlete's Foot is trying to look inconspicuous browsing the FemFresh options.

Liz   That woman really did fuck all favours for the sisterhood. I'm sure she's just a male-fantasist Mummy. But then so many things are . . .

'Men are born between a woman's legs and spend the rest of their life trying to get back there' – isn't that what they say?

Willow (*to audience*)   He's dropping the antifungal cream, and turning to go.

(*to* **Liz**) Can I /

Liz   Anyway, don't go believing it, my dear, children are not fulfilment! It's a blessing in disguise you can't have them.

Willow's *forehead lands on the counter.*

Liz   Christ, if all those blokes out there had been spending half their time wiping arses and mopping up sick, do you think they'd have invented or adventured to half the places round the world?

Willow (*to audience*)   He's on his way out, and I can see him hesitate and my whole body is aching for him to turn around.

Liz   But what am I saying, you already know this. You're a doctor and a scientist.

Willow (*to* **Liz**)   A pharmacist, not a doctor. (*To audience.*) And he's gone.

Liz   No, and thank god. When I was a child my mother and her friends used to call the local GP 'The Octopus'. He'd tell you to take all your clothes off for an ear infection. Terrible man. Dead now thankfully.

No, we don't need his type any more, hiding behind the desk. We need a new breed to sweep out the dead wood.

Willow   I just write for a scientific journal, that's all.

Liz   You're a writer? What are you writing about?

Willow   Trees. Medicinal properties of trees. I'm – It's – My articles have been commissioned as a book, that I'm trying to write.

Liz (*pause*)   Are you really?

Blimey, of all the things . . .

Liz is amazed and lost for words.

Willow   Yep. Studied biochemistry at university, did a Masters in 2009 and /

Liz   Then we need you.

Willow   Excuse me?

Liz   Yes. Tonight. On the vigil. You must come.

Willow *brings her head up from the counter.*

Willow   I'm sorry, I don't understand.

Liz   They're cutting down the trees! They are going to cut down the woods! My woods.

Our woods!

Willow   Who is going to/

Liz   The bloody council, of course! For some bullshit redevelopment, that we don't need but no doubt they are going to make some bloody money out of it. And they are cutting down *my* trees!

Willow   Redevelopment? Near here?

Liz   Yes!

Willow   Do you know what it's for?

Liz   Some bloody shopping centre and a car park or something.

Willow   It wasn't . . . Barvert Alliance was it?

Willow *begins to take the piece of paper she was given by her manager out of her pocket.*

Liz   How on earth did you know that?

Willow   That's the parent company that owns this place.

Liz   So?

Willow   They're building a megastore.

Liz   What?!

Willow   I just got offered a promotion. In the megastore.

Liz   But . . . but . . . but . . .

Willow   They're planning to capitalise on the NHS being under threat.

Liz   Are you sure?

Willow   That's the rumour.

Liz   Oh my god, we've got to get out there! We just can't let them just slice up our life like this! How can this be happening (*she is leaving to exit.* **Willow** *has stopped still*) Are you coming?

Willow   I, er – I.

Liz   Come on, what are you waiting for?

Willow   I can't just leave work!

Liz   They are going to cut down the trees and we need you!

Willow   I'm an *employee*.

Liz   Yes, but fuck that! We need a scientist who can stand up to them and quote proper research until they can't justify their selfish, money-grabbing, bastard little behaviour any more!

Willow   I can't go into the woods.

Liz   Nonsense! Of course you can.

Willow   No, no, I can't. I'm, er, in my work clothes, and –

Liz   You have to. This is the future we're talking about. I shall bring you something to change in to.

Willow   I can't. I –

Liz   There's a willow tree out there that my father planted when my older brother was born. Eighty-three years ago. And I'm not going to see it massacred!

Willow   A willow tree?

Liz   Yes, and it's healthier than I am.

Willow   *Eighty-three?* Are you *sure?*

Liz   Of course I'm sure! That lady and I have been through a lot, and she's always been there for me when I needed her, and I'm not about to let her down now.

Right. I'm going home, sorting out Jeremy and then I'll pick up what we need.

(*As she exits.*) Remember: Vive la Revolution, Willow! *Vulva* la Revolution!!

Exit **Liz**.

Willow *is left in a daze in the shop. Pause.*

Willow   I won't go.

I'll just slip out the back door and tell her I was busy or something. She doesn't need me.

Liz is just . . . she's lonely.

You don't confide in the someone you think is the 'shop girl' if you're not a bit . . . And you don't leave your husband in a utility room and need antidepressants and sleeping tablets, if you're not a bit . . .

But that thought scared me. I felt for her. I felt for her future, and . . . and . . . I wondered about mine.

A customer comes to the counter to buy painkillers.

Willow   Oh – er – hi there.

The customer puts three boxes on the counter.

Oh, sorry, you can only buy a maximum of 32 painkillers at one time.

(*To audience.*) I get a grunt and an eye roll.

Willow (*to customer*)   Just the aspirin then?

(*To customer.*) Did you know that aspirin comes from willow trees?

(*To audience.*) I get a dead-eyed stare.

(*To customer, she ploughs on, regardless.*) Yep, Salicylic acid – the stuff that numbs the pain – was first discovered from the bark of willow trees. Brew up a tea of willow bark and it can relieve headaches and bring down fevers. Fascinating, isn't it?

Pause as she looks for a reaction/interaction.

(*To audience.*) Nope, still nothing. He shoves them in his bag and there's a sort of cough-grunt that could be interpreted as a 'thank you', and he goes.

And I wonder, is that the most conversation he's had all day?

She weighs up her evening/decision ahead of her.

I thought of Liz's willow tree and their ability to numb the pain, even if only temporarily, and I thought . . .

Pause.

I have to know.

I have to know if it's healthy. I have to know *how* it's still alive.

So when she was standing there, (**Liz** *enters silently with a backpack on, a placard sticking out of it, and a pair of wellies in her hands*) outside the front of the shop, waiting, with an extra pair of wellington boots in her hand, (**Liz** *hands her a pair of wellies*)

I thought

Perhaps.

After all this time

Perhaps

It'll be okay.

Scene Eleven

Gap Dynamics.

Liz *and* **Willow** *in the woods, in the dark, slightly lost. The lights have echoes of* **Willow**'s *panic attack in Scene Six.*

Liz   Well this is embarrassing.
You see I normally walk in the mornings, so with the usual daylight saving crap, it's rather darker than I expected.
I'm sure it's here somewhere.

Willow   Look, honestly I believe you, I don't need to see it anymore.

Liz   The willow is just near a rather majestic old tree stump that I usually stop on. Which, from what you say about the root network, is probably still connected, even the dead ones still making a contribution. What a fabulous thought! To go out with one's boots on, as they say.

Willow   Yes, it's great, but it's a bit cold and I have an early start tomorrow.

Liz   No, no, no, just give me a minute, I'll find it!
Now is it that way . . . ?
Or that way . . . ?
Could do with a bloody torch though.

Willow (*using her phone for sat nav*)   Hang on, fuck no reception! How are we going to get out of here?

Liz   Oh don't worry! I'll find it in the end. Course it could be morning by then! (*She laughs.*) Well, we'll have had an adventure at least.

Willow *is beginning to panic.*

Willow   We need to leave.

Liz (*still searching*)   Oh no, bit of a mud bog that way, don't think that's the path.

Willow   This isn't safe.

Liz   Of course it is dear, I've walked these woods for over forty years. I just have to find this tree stump and I'll know the way from there.

Willow   You don't understand, I don't want/

Liz   Come on girl, think happy thoughts. Or think about wine, that's what I usually do.

Willow   I can't be in all these leaves.

Liz   Nope, briar patch that way. Well, bugger me.

Willow *is beginning to hyperventilate.*

Liz   Did we turn right at that bench back there, or left?

Willow *has sunk to her knees.*

Willow   . . . have to . . .

Liz   Are you okay? What's wrong?

Willow   I'm feeling unwell, yeah, I need to/

Liz   Breathe. In and out. Count it 1,2,3, and out 1,2,3, in 1,2,3, out 1,2,3,

Willow *begins to count and breathe.*

Liz   Can you sit down, darling? Would that help?

Willow *is still counting/breathing.*

Liz   Come on, let's sit down. That's it.

She guides **Willow** *to sit down.*

Liz   Why don't you try telling me about something that calms you. Come on. Tell me about how sociable trees are again. About the trees all being connected.

Willow *still can't talk. She's trying to say 'I feel sick'.*

There's a great big network, isn't there. Streaming beneath our feet with all these trees talking to each other through their roots, isn't there?

Willow *nodding, breathing.*

There's fungi in the soil that connects them, even the pioneer ones, out on the edge.

Willow *nods. She is starting to calm.*

Like willows? Willows can still be talked to, underground, by the other trees?

Willow   Should be.

Liz   That's it, good. Tell me another fact about trees.

Willow   They – um, there's a theory that – that trees can scream.

Liz   Good. That's interesting. How can they do that?

Willow   Ultrasonic. We can't hear it.

Liz   Go on.

Willow   In droughts. The flow of water up and down the tree. It's interrupted.

Pause.

The tree begins to vibrate. Like a scream for thirst.

Liz   In pain?

Willow   As a warning. To other trees. About the drought.

Liz   Or screaming for help?

Willow   Could be.

Liz   Gosh. (*Looking at a tree.*) You think you know someone, and you really just don't. (*Beat.*) Funny, we're taught at school it's all about competition, fighting for light and space and resources. Elbowing the other fellow out the way. Or branching them out the way, if you like. But that's not it, is it? That's just half the story.

It's actually all about

Willow & Liz (*simultaneously*)   Co-operation.

They smile.

Liz   Learn something new every day. And who would have thought, trees can talk!

Willow   It's taken scientists a long time to learn how to listen, though.

Liz   Well, that's nothing new, dear. So many people don't know how to listen. It's a skill in itself.

Willow   You seem quite good at it.

Liz   Learnt that from you, dear. In the shop. All that time you give to people. Even an old woman who doesn't know what she's talking about half the time!

She winks and nudges her.

Willow *smiles.*

Willow Thanks, I'm feeling a bit better now.

Liz Just give me a minute to rest these old bones and I'll ferret our way out in no time, don't worry. You must sign a copy of your book for me when it comes out.

Beat.

Willow If it ever comes out. Having a bit of problem with the writing at the moment.

Liz Oh dear, what's happening?

Willow I just . . . well, I keep getting sidelined talking about wild cherry trees, and not really staying on track.

Small pause before she can admit her failing.

It's kind of derailing the book, if I'm honest.

Liz Are they not medicinal?

Willow Well . . . well . . . I suppose, they could be. I hadn't really thought of that.

It's one of the unsolved mysteries of forestry, how wild cherry trees manage to block self-pollination. They can test the incoming pollen and dry up the tube if it matches its own DNA.

Liz Stopping inbreeding?

Willow Yes, in a nutshell.

Liz Blimey! Are you going to solve the mystery and go down in scientific history? Jolly good on you girl, we need more women up there among all the crusty old men in white coats.

Willow Oh um, no I didn't really think of that.

Liz   But . . . You never struck me as the discovery type, though, you know?

Willow   What do you mean?

Liz   Well, I always imagined such scientists needed that look of burning pursuit of curiosity at the expense of all others, but you're . . . well, you seem too caring and . . . well, *nurturing* for that kind of selfishness.

But then, I suppose they do say 'Necessity is the mother of invention'. Is there a necessity for this discovery?

Pause.

Willow   You know, it's quite late. (*Getting up.*) Won't your husband be wondering where you are?

Short pause.

Liz   Jeremy's taking care of himself this evening.

Short pause.

Willow   It's just I need to get some work done /

Liz   Oh dear, have I put my foot in it again?

Willow   Oh, no, it's not that. It's just I just want to go, you know? I'm tired and, um . . . Thank you very much for the boots, I can give them back to you when /

Liz   I don't care about the boots, I'm worried about you Willow. About you and the trees and why you?

Willow (*caught off guard*)   What?

Liz   Why wild cherry trees?

Willow   –

Liz   I may be old but the memory's still there, dear. You told me you had blocked tubes.

I remember. I could see it upset you. I think it's upsetting you now – you've got the same face on.

Willow *has begun to cry.*

Liz   Why are you stuck on wild cherry trees, Willow?

Silence.

Liz   Why do you need to know about blocked tubes [and inbreeding], Willow?

Tears run down **Willow***'s face.* **Liz** *waits.*

Willow   Because they are very important and could help so many people –

Pause.

So many things.

Long pause. She is crying a lot. **Liz** *lets* **Willow** *cry and then comes over to her carefully and holds her.*

Liz   That's it. Come on. Let it out. That's it. Let it out.

Willow *cries.*

Willow   When I was kid I – always stayed for the holidays at my nan's house, we'd all go together. She had a big garden and a wood close by. I –

Nan's house was –
It had a living room with three massive armchairs.
I used to curl up in them and watch hours of TV.

With him.
He would be official babysitter when Nan went out.
She used to mutter something about 'church group'
but I'm pretty sure it was Mecca Bingo.

He was much older but
He'd watch Cartoon Network with us
and he was really good at impressions of the Rugrats.
He'd save a space for me and I'd wriggle in next to him.
And I started to feel things in my body.
A hint of adrenaline.
I grew to really like it,
to crave it.

I wanted to be close to him.

The day it happened we were playing forty forty in and out of the trees

Liz   Great game.

Willow   Mmm.

Liz   Sorry, go on.

Willow   I knew those trees better than all of them.
So I ran out further than anyone.
He ran after me and I –
When he took hold of my forearms, and I fell down, I was falling
My dress pulled up around my face.
The wet leaves soaking into my body, covering my mouth, I couldn't breathe –
The smell of the leaves –

Pause.

I didn't make a sound. I barely cried.

Pause.

The leaves were in my clothes and my hair and Mum told me off for not looking after my dress properly, my tights were ripped and my shoes caked in mud.

Pause.

I tried to tell her that it was (*she can't say it*) him but she thought I meant the mud and said 'nobody likes a tattle-tale, Willow'.

Liz   Who?

Willow   I can't, it doesn't matter who.

Liz   Yes, it does.

Pause.

Willow   I've never told anyone – [this]

My brother.

Liz   –

Pause.

Willow   I bled . . . There were bruises – everywhere.

Pause.

Liz   I understand.

Willow   He was a lot older than me.
From my dad's first marriage.
He'd been living with my dad because he'd been kicked out
by his mum.
Soon left my dad's too.
Never saw him again after that.

But I'm reminded of him every day. Every day when I look
at my body and know that he poisoned me. Every day.

She looks at **Liz**.

Salpingitis. That's why I can't have children.
The tubes are blocked from the scars because the infection
he gave me went undetected for so long.

She cries softly.

Liz   Let it out. Let it out, dear.

Willow   Wild cherry trees, have worked this out, stopping
the poison. I mean for fuck's sake. I won't ever carry my own
children. I'm the Hollow Willow. I'm the fucking secret
keeper, the empty tree.

She cries. Long pause.

Liz *gets out her vape and starts vaping.*

Liz   You know, motherhood is so much more than carrying
a baby in your womb. That's just . . . germination, I suppose.

I don't think motherhood really starts until the child is in
your arms.

Willow *looks at her.*

Liz   I think motherhood is the ability to empty yourself out and put the child first. They have such voracious needs and putting your own emotions aside can be much more challenging than just making space in your body.

I didn't really do it for Oscar. Fighting such a battle with my own demons, I didn't know how.

It sounds like you've been fighting your demons on your own for too long. I think you need to break the silence but perhaps this book isn't really doing it for you.

Willow   Maybe I should be writing about something else.

Liz   Maybe so.

Willow   Maybe I should write about . . . about infertility after . . . after –

Liz *nods*.

Liz   Write about it, talk about it, sing and dance about it – anything you like about it, really. The time for silence is over.

Willow   Yes. The time for silence is over.

She blows her nose.

God, I don't think my editor is going to be pleased with that!

Liz   Fuck 'im! It is a *Him*, I suppose?

Willow   Yes it is.

Liz   My friend Sarah had therapy, you know. It was all hush hush, therapy was a dirty word in those days, but she came out of it a new woman. Left the WI and everything. Moved away. Pity, she was the only real friend I had. Those with demons tend to be far more interesting than those who have never suffered.

And more compassionate, I sometimes think.

It's why you're so terribly good at your job, Willow.

Willow   Oh. I /

Liz   I've seen you, every day at that pharmacy. You don't give people judgement. You give them compassion. And that is the greatest love you could give.

Willow   Thank you.

Liz   I'm sorry that boy hurt you.

Willow

Liz   And I'm sorry you've suffered in silence for so long.

Willow   I probably need to go and talk to someone about it. Get some help.

Liz   That's it! Open up, break out of the silent imprisonment.

Pause.

No idea how women have learnt to be silent for so long. Such a waste of all these amazing lives that could have been.

Pause.

Willow   What are you being silent about?

Liz   Oh . . .

Pause.

The time I cut off one of my sister's blonde plaits because I was jealous.

The dog food I added to the WI's lasagna bake because they were all judging me for my mild flirtations with their starved-of-affection husbands.

All sorts of things I'm sure.

Shall we say, our roots are intertwined, you and I, Willow. But that's for another day, I'm sure.

Pause. She holds **Willow**'s *hand.*

We need to shake off these leaves and get going, as you say.

Liz *steps forward out of the scene into a pool of light, alone.*

Scene Twelve

Crowning.

The lighting changes. **Liz** *steps forward.*

Liz (*to audience*)   I was glad to have been able to help.

Here was this (*she searches for the word*) *child* hurting in front of me, and I managed to help.

I listened and
Made space. For her.
Perhaps I hadn't totally failed at motherhood after all.

We may not have found our way to the protest that night but we rebelled against a different kind of system instead. A system of thousands of years of silencing.

Of course, if you've been through something similar yourself, you can . . . External bruises can heal but somehow internal ones feel like they never do.
I realised that, listening to Willow. Making space for truths we don't want to hear. And somehow, I heard my own.

I don't think Jeremy had ever really meant to do it, that night he found my Pill. He'd been to feed the horses with Oscar.
And that's how he smelt. Animal.

We used to call it 'him getting what he wanted' which is ridiculous really. Because we were married it wasn't rape. Not till the 1990s anyway.

We barely touched each other since that time.
Spent our lives hopping in and out of other lovers' beds, and agreeing by mutual silence that it was never to be discussed.
And then I washed and dressed him,
Every day,
as if we'd been kind and tender all those years. What a farce.

A farce, from which he has taken his final bow.

I'd been stockpiling all these wonderful pills the doctors
positively throw at you, once you tell them you're depressed
and can't sleep.
Anything not to have to actually pay the expense of a human
being for you to talk to. I am finally free. I am finally free of
the drudgery!

That's why women are conditioned to be silent, I think.
Because they wouldn't take it otherwise.
They wouldn't take the household slavery

And the abuse that it takes to be a new mother.
The sleep deprivation, the constant screaming and the
availability of your body for someone else's needs at no
matter what cost to you!
They wouldn't take it.

They'd rebel.

And that's what I want to do now!
I don't know whether to dance or cry.
Something in me wants to explode!

The black rot was lighter for a time walking in the woods
with Willow. I felt alive again, purposeful, bearing fruit.
And now I want to blow it up for good! Set off a million
fireworks or . . . dance naked down Broadway . . . or climb
Everest just to plant a fucking great flag on the top of it with
my face on it saying
'Liz was here! She LIVED!'
She didn't die that day of the fork in the road, aged 18 in a
chemist in Hurtmore!

Sweet eighteen-year-old Liz (*she thinks fondly of her young self*)
who knew how to light up the world with her dreams and
schemes. How I want to be her again! Just one last time.

What would eighteen-year-old Liz have done?

That's what I keep thinking.

What would she do?

Liz *steps back into the scene with* **Willow** *and the lighting returns to
the woods of Scene 11.*

Scene Eleven (2)

Fruits

Willow   I hate leaves.

Liz *kicks a pile of leaves and sends them flying.*

Liz   Just leaves dear.

Willow   I guess they just remind me of . . .

Pause.

Liz   Silencing?

Willow   Suffocation, I was going to say.

Pause.

Same thing maybe.

Liz   Nothing in leaves but the weight we give them.

Liz *kicks another pile of leaves. She walks round the stage sending up flurries of leaves.*

When I was younger, my greatest ambition was to be Fred Astaire. Did I tell you that? People always used to ask me, 'Why not Ginger Rogers?' but why be the follower, when you could be the choreographer and create the steps yourself?

I learnt all the steps and danced the routines in top hat and tails, even though they told me it wasn't feminine! Whatever that bloody well means. Covering yourself in make up and being a mute, pretty little doll? Fuck that shit.

You made me realise that, Willow. With your questions. We weren't taught to question it.

It was all 'Don't be a show off Liz, don't have an opinion, don't tell the truths that burn, don't kick and scream and light things up.'
I've had enough of that now.

*She begins to dance, through the leaves, the footsteps of Fred
Astaire's 'Puttin on the Ritz'.* **Willow** *takes out her phone and puts
on 'Black Horse and The Cherry Tree' by KT Tunstall. The two
women dance through the leaves together in a great moment of
release. Towards the end* **Liz** *jumps on the counter, and* **Willow**
pulls a graffiti can out of her back pack and throws it to her. **Liz**
catches it and then climbs on **Willow**'s *shoulders and they make their
way over to the 'Boots' sign, giggling and laughing uproariously
and ridiculously.* **Liz** *'graffities' over the BOOTS sign with a big 'R'
so it becomes 'ROOTS'. Blackout.*)

Acknowledgements

When Jess emailed me in autumn 2017 asking me to co-write *Boots* I didn't know quite what I was 'in' for. *Boots* has been an amazing journey to write but also an incredible story of trust and friendship. I am honoured that Jess asked me to be part of this unforgettable journey.

As *Boots* was written so, also, was the MeToo movement writing itself into our collective consciousness. The movement is a revolution of storytelling. Histories, Herstories and so many people's stories that have never been told before. They have been whispered, silenced and shamed but now these stories are beginning to be recognised. This is a revolution of recognition, and, as we know, all revolutions need to start with a rebellion.

Boots is the story of a rebellion. It is a rebellion against the silencing of so many thousands of years. It is a questioning of our entrenched codes of conduct, repeated and unchallenged for so long. Willow and Liz, the two characters of *Boots*, make each other question their conditioning and their lives of silence.

Together, in their connection, they create a slow revolution. A revolution of kindness. Of consideration, time, trust and friendship. Listening, caring, hearing people speak, having the courage to tell our stories and the assurance that they will be treated with respect, is the revolution we need. In that everyday-way, like Willow and Liz, we can recognise a whole world in someone on the other side of the counter to us.

Boots at The Bunker was only made possible by the fantastic team who work there, most especially Chris Sonnex, David Ralf and our outstanding dramaturg Debbie Hannan. Thank you Nadia Papachronopoulou for your unfailing commitment and belief in the script. Thank you Alexandra Graham for being, as ever, a rock. Thank you to all the actors who have read, reflected on and given input into the making of Liz and Willow, they are wonderful women because they are made of all those wonderful women. Thank you Rosalind Campbell for your inspiration and your friendship, and thank you Jane Tapp, Tara Malcolm, Dr Miriam Leonard, Dr Emma Trunchion, Dr Edward Tapp and Hope Williams for your support. Thank you Dom and Anna at Methuen, thanks to Dr Andrea Wigfield from The Centre for Loneliness Studies and ACE for supporting this production and Dr Madeline Castro for your wonderful thought and insight.

Finally, thank you to my mother Harriet whose input, support and appreciation for *Boots* is beyond words. Thank you Toren Tapp for being the sweet-souled source of inspiration and solace that you are, and thank you William Tapp for making all things possible.

Sacha Voit, 2019

* * *

At some point in December of 2016 I stood behind a 70 something year old woman in Boots the chemist whilst she asked for different pills, creams and products. She was being served by a kind, intelligent pharmacist and there was something about the transaction that made me think. I tried to write a poem about it, but it was terrible, so I tried to forget about it. I couldn't; both these people stayed with me.

In January 2017 I met Tanya Loretta Dee. We had been cast opposite each other in Sabrina Mahfouz and Hollie McNish's play *Offside*. Tanya played a footballer called Mickey. I played a footballer called Keeley. Mickey and Keeley told a beautiful story about football and friendship. Within a week of rehearsals, I realised that Tanya was not only one of the finest actors I have ever met, but one of the finest people. She taught me so much during our rehearsals and months on tour. *Offside* ended up at the Edinburgh Festival in the summer of 2017. Tanya, Daph (our wonderful third cast member) and I proceeded to have one of the most hilarious months of my life. I was not drinking for the first time in many years and was so grateful to be with these two. Who needs booze when you've got amazing friends. We laughed and laughed. We also cried. Life happened at us and we had many long conversations about it.

With my new found sobriety I realised I could get more work done. During that August I applied to VAULT festival with my first play, *Sparks*. I was terrified. One evening I sent the script to Tanya. She read it over night and installed in me the confidence to continue and apply to the festival. Had she not shown me such love, care and strength, I may never have done it. Simultaneously, I had begun thinking about *Boots* again. Having now worked and talked with Tanya for nearly a year, I realised that this story was related to her. It was for her.

We decided to apply to the festival. We sat in Tad, my favourite Turkish restaurant, and wrote the application. I texted Phil Scott-Wallace to see if he would produce it and he said yes, immediately. At this point I had written three scenes and two monologues and had almost no idea what the story would be. We waited. And found out a few weeks later that we had got in. I had a period of huge elation followed by what could only be described as very, very intense panic.

We were in to the festival, but I had not written the play. I walked home one night realising how little time I had. I started writing the character of Liz first. She was written for the actress Illona Linthwaite who did the original R&D and VAULT festival production. Illona taught me how to tell stories. Her trust in my writing and acting has helped me in more ways than I can describe. Thank you Illona for inspiring Liz and finding her voice and heart.

I was really struggling to find the story and even to begin to know how to do it. One evening, I was walking home late and realised exactly what I had to do. I had to get Sacha Voit to write it with me. Sacha and I had written together for the Bush Bazaar years ago and we had laughed so much. We also have always understood how each other's minds work. I emailed Sacha late that night asking if we could work together on this. It was a long email full of many things. I sent it and lay on my bedroom floor. Within two minutes, a reply, with two excellent words; 'I'm in.' I cried with relief. We then proceeded to write *Boots* in six weeks. I would sit on Sacha's sitting room floor while we worked out the plot and talked at length about Liz and Willow. Sacha found the links and words, and made it what it is. I am so grateful for Sacha's brain, kindness and perseverance. Sacha has taken the reins on this project and has done all the rewrites for the run at The Bunker, whilst also making the most brilliant ACE application.

This play is a result of the power and brilliance of female friendship.

The VAULT festival run was very generously supported by Paul Mulholland. Who remains one of the truest and kindest friends and supporters I have ever had. The VAULT run was also made possible by the following kind, thoughtful people who donated to our Crowdfunder. A huge thank you to Flair May, Tomas Coombes, Jennie Eggleton, Emma Brooke, Leena Ceccolini, Colin Hubbard, Estacia, Karen and Erik Michel, Judy Duff, Barry Assinder, Yvonne Angulo, Izo Fitzroy, Ruth Penfold, Lizzie Vogler, Dan Avery, Emma O'Connor, Steve Batchelor, Stuart Gibbs, Miriam Kidane, Anneka Harry, Stephen Shapiro, Charlotte Chinn, Mat Burt, Richard Corgan, Natasha Shaikh, Ty Powell, Jessica Sweidan, Jayne Buxton, Alannah Bascombe, Jade Anouka, Pauline Chinn, Cristina Saretti, Sabrina Mahfouz, Ruth Hughes, Ray Cape, Noah Ball, Geraldine Wright, Caroline Bryant, Dan Lehner, Lucinda Burgess, Jamie Potter, mmlbl, sachdog and Judy Duff.

My thanks also to Lucy Wray, Phil Scott-Wallace, Jack Wyllie and Catherine Morgan for their work on the VAULT run.

My final thanks goes to VAULT Festival who gave us the space and the trust to try this play out. And, lastly, my future husband, Mat Burt, who helped and helps me make everything possible.

Jessica Butcher, 2019